The Way of The Word

Contemplative Reflections on the Gospels

William C. Martin

PRESS

Book design by David Skinner

All Scripture references are from *The New Jerusalem Bible*, published by Doubleday, New York, NY.

CTS Press
P.O. Box 520
Decatur, GA 30031

Introduction

I hesitate to write an introduction because it requires more words when my goal is to point to the Word Itself, which is so often hidden by words.

This book grew out of responses to my book, *The Art of Pastoring* (CTS Press, ISBN 1-885121-00-8). In that book I attempted to present the insights of Lao Tzu's classic *Tao Te Ching* in a format that would be helpful to professional clergy. I must have touched a nerve, for I have received many requests from clergy and laity alike to expand upon that material by showing how the simple, direct, non-linear style of Taoist thought can be seen in the writings of the Christian Gospels. This book, *The Way of the Word*, represents my attempt to answer these requests.

The response of the soul to words on a page causes the miracle of the living Word—the Word written on the heart. My words are attempts to record the response of my own soul to the recorded words of Jesus. Somewhere between the lines of his words and my soul's responses lies the dancing, breathing, living Word incarnate.

The living Word does not reside in my words, of course. But neither does it reside in a perfunctory reading of the words of Jesus. Words are just words unless a spark of divine energy jumps from mind to soul within the hearer.

The living Word does not lie in a series of doctrinal points outlined by scholars and preachers of the faith, helpful though their words might be. Nor does it lie in the ink patterns on a page, no matter how cherished those ink patterns might be. It does not lie in what other people say you should believe or think, however good their intentions might be.

The living Word is found in the deepest, most fundamental part of your being when it senses the truth. This is the Word that was in the beginning with God. This is the Word that was in Jesus. This is the Word that still dances in the cosmos creating, birthing, and bringing life. And this is the Word within your own soul, teaching you what no external teacher can: who you really are and what you really believe.

This book is an invitation to a life of trust—trust that the Word will accomplish its mission within you; trust that your heart knows the truth once you are able to listen, truly listen, to it; and trust that such knowing will truly set you free.

I hope you use this little book in many ways. I have included a meditation for each week of the year, in case you wish to live with each scripture and thought for that period of time. Skim through the book if you wish, picking out those thoughts that capture your attention. Live with these for a while and experiment with making the breath prayers part of your spiritual practice.

A word about breath prayers

These short phrases are designed to be silent or spoken prayers in rhythm with your breathing. As you breathe in, repeat the first phrase, and as you breathe out, repeat the second. Continue this rhythmic praying for as long as you wish. Breath prayers are among the oldest of Christian devotional practices. This simple technique enables the one who prays to move from the realm of complicated word and thought patterns into the realm of silence and quiet of the mind. The "monkey chatter" that occupies so much of our mind becomes replaced by a single devotional thought. Eventually this thought becomes embedded deep in the subconscious mind and begins to change our perspective on every area of life.

The prayer may be used for a regular period of meditation but also helps restore the soul at odd times during the day: while sitting in traffic jams, waiting in lines, or fretting during anxious moments.

Many spiritual directors recommend picking one breath prayer and sticking with it for months or even years. I feel that using a variety of prayers is more helpful. As you work your way through this book, I hope that some of the prayer suggestions may become part of the transformation of your thinking. Many who have used an earlier edition of this book report that using one meditation as a focus for five to fifteen minutes once a day for a week—coupled with the use of the corresponding breath prayer throughout the day—serves as an effective contemplative discipline.

However you choose to use the meditations and prayers, I hope that they serve as simple pointers to the Divine Lover whose love for each of us surpasses all understanding.

Blessings,

Bill Martin
Phoenix, Arizona
July, 1997

Contents

Meditations		Scripture	Page

For Nancy,
as usual.

Meditation 1 - Pointing

No one can explain the Word
for the word that can be explained
is not the Eternal Word.

No one can describe the Way
for the way that can be described
is not the Eternal Way.

Your teachers can only point.
And when they point,
for heaven's sake
stop looking at their finger!

Reflections

This is not a book of answers. Mere words cannot fully communicate answers. All words are pointers to the heart. Find your heart. There you will find your answers.

Breath Prayer 1

Breathe in:
"Point the way ..."
Breathe out:
"... I will follow."

He would not speak to them
except in parables.

(Mark 4:34)

Meditation 2 - Sight

When sight is clarified
by an understanding of the Word,
wherever you look, you see God.
Whatever the eyes perceive,
whether judged by the mind beautiful
or ugly,
is seen by the soul
as a sign of God.

To see the light,
do not try to believe
certain things
about light.
Merely open your eyes.

Reflections

Pay attention! Stop sleep walking. Whenever a situation seems dark to you it is because you haven't yet learned how to see. Light and dark are the same to God. Open your eyes. Wider, wider.

Breath Prayer 2

Breathe in:
"Open my eyes ..."
Breathe out:
"... that I might see."

"Whoever believes in me believes not in me but in the one who sent me, and whoever sees me, sees the one who sent me. I have come into the world as light, to prevent anyone who believes in me from staying in the dark any more."

(John 12:44-46)

Meditation 3 - One

God is whole,
undivided,
One.

We have made categories,
judgments,
divisions.

God uttered,
"One!"
We have declared,
"Many!"
and have created
a world of suffering.

God still whispers,
"One."
If you become very still,
you will hear your heart echo,
"One!"

Reflections

You don't need to make the categories of "us" and "them." You really don't. Don't be afraid of one another. It is the delight of God that one day we all recognize that we, though unique individuals, are one body in Christ.

Breath Prayer 3

Breathe in:
"Only ..."
Breathe out:
"... One!"

[In praying for his followers Jesus said,] "May they all be one, just as Father, you are in me and I am in you, so that they also may be in us ...that they may be one as we are one."

(John 17:21,22)

Meditation 4 - Child

The mind creates many gods,
and many ways of seeking status
in their eyes.
The mind is terribly mistaken.
There is only one
God,
and one human status:
Child.

Reflections
Why are you making it so complicated? It's really very simple.
You are God's child. Period!

Breath Prayer 4

Breathe in:
"I am ..."
Breathe out:
"... God's child."

**"Go and find my brothers, and tell them:
I am ascending to my Father and your Father,
to my God and your God."**

(John 20:17)

Meditation 5 - Seeing and Believing

There are two ways of seeing:
with the eyes,
and with the heart.
Eyes respond to light waves
between 400 and 800 nanometers.
Most of the electromagnetic spectrum
lies outside of these boundaries,
and cannot be seen by eyes.
Only the heart has the capacity
to know beyond seeing.
Trust what the heart knows,
not the tiny bit the eyes see.

Reflections

Which of us is seeing "reality"? What does "reality" really look like? Be careful of using that old crutch, "I believe what I see." You don't see much.

Breath Prayer 5

Breathe in:
"I see ..."
Breathe out:
"... with my heart."

**"You believe because you can see me.
Blessed are those who have not seen and yet believe."**

(John 20:29)

Meditation 6 - Words

The foolish man comes to words about Jesus
thinking he is coming to life.
He persists in looking outside himself for Jesus
thinking he will find Him out there.
He refuses to turn to the inner way,
afraid to look at the mystery of his soul.

He spends his life thinking that
his Jesus words,
and his Jesus thoughts,
and his Jesus concepts
will substitute for the Christ-Life
waiting within,
waiting for the words to cease.

Reflections

It is sometimes necessary to take a vacation from reading Scripture. Don't be shocked. Do you really think that you cannot make an idol out of the Bible and your religious words? Try this. For a whole week, do not read the Bible, pray, or speak any religious words. Just pay close attention to everything that is before you. Be quiet. Watch. Listen. Whenever you feel tempted to say or do anything religious, resist it. Then return to your reading and praying and let your words find their proper place.

Breath Prayer 6

Breathe in:
"Christ is ..."
Breathe out:
"... within me."

---

*"You pour over the scriptures believing that in them
you can find eternal life...yet you refuse to come
to me to receive life."*

(John 5:39,40)

Meditation 7 - Writings

> *Throughout the ages men and women*
> *have found God in their heart,*
> *and have written of their discovery*
> *with stumbling words*
> *and imperfect metaphors.*
> *But when a person of the Word*
> *reads their words,*
> *heart touches heart*
> *and God is discovered anew,*
> *beyond words.*

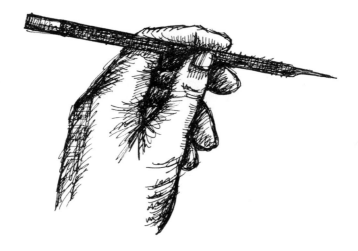

Reflections

When you read the Scriptures listen for the heart of the writer. It was in his or her heart that the Word of God was active. The heart of the person behind the words is the dwelling place of the living God. Read for the heart.

Breath Prayer 7

Breathe in:
"From your heart ..."
Breathe out:
"... to my heart."

**"If you really believed (Moses) you would believe me too,
since it was about me that he was writing."**

(John 5:46)

Meditation 8 - Kingdom

The Kingdom,
and the power,
and the glory,
are inner realities.

If someone comes to you
with news of the Kingdom
in the outer world,
Run to the hills!
Run for your life!

Reflections
How can you build an eternal kingdom out of temporary stuff?
An eternal kingdom can only be built out of eternal stuff.

Breath Prayer 8

Breathe in:
"The Kingdom is ..."
Breathe out:
"... inside of me."

"Jesus, as he realized they were about to come and take him by force and make him king, fled back to the hills alone."

(John 6:15)

If you are looking for one to teach you
and be your guide in the way of the Word,
do not look in great buildings.
Avoid magnificent churches.
Do not be misled by numerous programs
attracting crowds of people.

The one who will be your teacher
will sit face to face with you
and with quiet simplicity
will point you to your soul.

Reflections

Large vital churches with an abundance of programs can be helpful. But the serious business of your own soul's guidance requires a deeper relationship.

Breath Prayer 9

Breathe in:
"Show me ..."
Breathe out:
... my soul."

"In all truth I tell you, you are looking for me not
because you have seen the signs, but because
you have had all the bread
you wanted to eat."

(John 6:26)

Meditation 10 - Harvest

The world would teach
that life must be preserved.
The Word would teach
that life must be harvested.

Sun and rain,
compost and manure,
root and stalk,
seed and flower.
When the time for harvest comes,
the plant rejoices.
For this moment
it was grown.

Reflections

You are growing toward harvest. Do not let that dismay you. Let it encourage you. What can you do today to grow toward a mature harvest? Remember it lies not in what you accomplish but in what you become.

Breath Prayer 10

Breathe in:
"I am ..."
Breathe out:
"... your harvest."

**"The harvest is rich but the laborers are few,
so ask the Lord of the harvest to send
laborers to do his harvesting."**

(Luke 10:2)

Meditation 11 - Accomplishment

Enjoy your work,
but do not think
that you have achieved something.
There is nothing for you to achieve.
God is.
You are.
That is enough.

Reflections

Do your work well today, but do not do it with a sense of pressure and tension. Let your muscles relax as you set the world, which has been riding on your shoulders, gently down. As you count your blessings this evening, do not consider what you have accomplished today; although that is not a bad thing, consider instead the simple fact that you are. It is in noticing that fact that you notice God.

Breath Prayer 11

Breathe in:
"God is ..."
Breathe out:
"... I am."

"Do not rejoice that the spirits submit to you;
rejoice instead that your names are written in heaven."

(Luke 10:20)

Meditation 12 - Wisdom

The curriculum of the Word
is not like that of school.
The more facts you learn,
the less you know.
The more you laugh and play,
the wiser you become,
until one day
your soul becomes light enough
to float into heaven.

Reflections

I am concerned in this era of the Internet that information is substituting for wisdom. Have you heard the phrase, "Information is power"? Don't believe it. Information is the illusion of power. Power is in the soul and is expressed as wisdom. Are you growing more wise?

Breath Prayer 12

Breathe in:
"Enlighten my mind ..."
Breathe out:
"... lighten my soul."

**"I bless you, Father, Lord of heaven and earth, for hiding
these things from the learned and the clever
and revealing them to little children."**

(Luke 10:21)

Meditation 13 - Imitation

If you imitate religious people
all you will become is
religious.
If you imitate successful people,
all you will become is
successful.
But if you imitate compassionate people
you will become like
God.

Reflections

Your heroes tell a great deal about your priorities. As you think about the qualities you admire in other people you might consider whether or not they are truly God-like qualities or just culturally approved qualities. Consider the place sports heroes occupy in our popularity polls.

Breath Prayer 13

Breathe in:
"Make me ..."
Breathe out:
"... like you."

[After telling the story of the good Samaritan,]
Jesus said to him, "Go and do the same yourself."

(Luke 10:37)

Meditation 14 - Beloved

A man and a woman do not marry
so there will be food on the table.
They marry so their love
will warm their nights
and delight their days.

If you become obsessed with your role
as servant of God,
you will become too busy
to be God's Beloved.

Reflections

There are many names for God. Consider for a moment the names God might have for you: "Beloved, lover, darling, child, sweetheart, honey, lamb, dear, . . ." If you are uncomfortable imagining God speaking these names to you, you might reconsider your images. There is no identity God desires more for you than "Beloved."

Breath Prayer 14

Breathe in:
"I am ..."
Breathe out:
"... beloved."

[At the home of Mary and Martha, Jesus spoke to the overly busy Martha,] "Martha, Martha, you worry and fret about so many things and yet few are needed, indeed only one. It is Mary who has chosen the better part, and it is not to be taken from her."

(Luke 10:41,42)

Meditation 15 - Focus

That on which you focus,
you become.
If you focus on the temporary
and illusory,
your life will become
a temporary
illusion.
If you focus on the eternal,
the real,
you will live forever.

Reflections
If you were to chart the things that occupy your mind for a whole day and list them under two columns: Temporary and Eternal, which column would be longer? Which are you becoming?

Breath Prayer 15

Breathe in:
"Clarify ..."
Breathe out:
"... my sight."

"The lamp of your body is your eye. When your eye is clear, your whole body, too, is filled with light; but when it is diseased, your body, too, will be darkened."

(Luke 11:34)

Meditation 16 - Inside

When good behavior is demanded,
evil retreats to the heart
where no one will see.
When a pure heart is sought,
evil withers
for it has no place to go.

Reflections

I am truly tired of hearing complaints about the behavior of all of the "thems" of our society. "They are doing thus and so. Isn't it terrible?" Or, "They are undermining our values. We have to stop them." Stop being concerned about behavior and seek to be at home in your own heart. It is there you will find God and it is from there that all good behavior will flow. And it's only *your* behavior that you are concerned with, right?

Breath Prayer 16

Breathe in:
"Make my heart ..."
Breathe out:
"... a place of love."

[When speaking to religious leaders who criticized
him for not ritually washing before a meal, Jesus said,]
"You Pharisees! You clean the outside of cup and plate,
while inside yourselves you are filled with extortion
and wickedness."

(Luke 11:39)

Meditation 17 - Teachers

Do not advertise yourself as a teacher.
You are not a teacher
until a student chooses
to make you one.
When a student makes this choice,
both of you together
will enter the kingdom.

<u>Reflections</u>

Is there someone in your life right now who is to be your teacher?
Notice carefully. It may not be obvious. Is there someone who is
to be your student? Be open, but not presumptive.

Breath Prayer 17

Breathe in:
"Teach me ..."
Breathe out:
"... in all I see."

[In speaking to teachers of religion, Jesus said,]
"Alas for you lawyers who have taken away the key of
knowledge! You have not gone in yourselves and have
prevented others going in who wanted to."

(Luke 11:52)

Meditation 18 - Testing God

If you pray
because you believe prayer "works,"
you are greatly mistaken.
God does not jump to your command,
nor is God in your employ.

Pray as one who
irrigates thirsty crops.
Such a one opens the water-gates,
steps aside,
and lets the water do
what water does.

One does not beg.
One does not push.
One does not worry.
Water flows.

Reflections

When you next sit, stand, or kneel to pray, relax the muscles in your face, soften your eyes, let the tension drain from your shoulders, open your hands, quiet your mind and stop begging.

Breath Prayer 18

Breathe in:
"I rest ..."
Breathe out:
"... and wait for you."

"Do not put the Lord your God to the test."

(Luke 4:12)

Meditation 19 - Blind

There is no reason to correct
another person's journey.
You cannot see their road clearly,
nor can they see yours.
If you pay close attention
you may see clearly
your own next step.
This is enough.
If you attempt to see another's
next step
you are greatly deluded.
Watch your step.

Reflections

Who are you trying to straighten out? Can you really see that clearly? Are you watching your own step?

Breath Prayer 19

Breathe in:
"My path is mine ..."
Breathe out:
"... your path is yours."

"Can one blind person guide another?
Surely both will fall into a pit."

(Luke 6:39)

Meditation 20 - Dancing

> *This is the path to God:*
> *When you are joyful,*
> *dance!*
> *When you are sad,*
> *cry.*
> *When you fast,*
> *feel God in your hunger.*
> *When you eat,*
> *taste God in your food.*
> *When you drink,*
> *swallow God with your wine.*

Reflections

Whatever you are doing, do it! If you are reading this book now, don't do anything else. Sit here and read it. If you are not going to give it your full attention, get up and do something else and give it your full attention. Stop thinking ahead. Live this moment! Now!

Breath Prayer 20

Breathe in:
"I laugh God ..."
Breathe out:
"... I cry God"

"For John the Baptist has come, not eating bread,
not drinking wine, and you say, 'He is possessed.'
The Son of man has come, eating and drinking,
and you say, 'Look, a glutton and a drunkard.'"

(Luke 7:33,34)

Meditation 21 - Flowing

When the fullness of the Word
touches a receptive vessel,
a flow occurs
that can be likened
to a river long contained
behind a dam,
whose water now is rushing
through the suddenly opened gates,
cascading home into the sea.

The person of the Word
is both the reservoir
and the river bed,
being filled
that it might empty
and be refilled
yet again.

Reflections

Stop thinking of your life as a struggle up a mountain. It is the
flow of a river home to the sea. No obstacle can possibly stop you
from completing the journey. Take a deep breath and let the river
flow. Feel it?

Breath Prayer 21

Breathe in:
"Power of God ..."
Breathe out:
"... flow through me."

[Referring to the woman who touched his cloak
and was healed, Jesus said,] "Somebody touched me.
I felt that power had gone out from me."

(Luke 8:46)

Meditation 22 - Taste

Can you see the kingdom?
Can you wash your hands
and feel the water's purity?
Can you use the toilet
and understand the wonder of your body?
Can you eat
and truly taste your food?
Can you watch a child
and see the play of God?
Can you see suffering
and know your heart's compassion?
Can you do your work
and pay it full attention?
Can you rest
and still your mind completely?
If you can learn to do
these things,
you will see the kingdom of God.
And when you taste death,
you will swallow it up.

Reflections

Anyone can eat a meal. Not everyone can taste it. When you eat your next meal ask yourself, "Am I tasting this food?" Learning to really pay attention to all aspects of life will reduce the fear of death. To the person who is truly alive to the ordinary moments of life, death becomes just one more experience to be fully digested. It is this full attention that reveals the kingdom of God within the experience.

Breath Prayer 22

Breathe in:
"I taste ..."
Breathe out:
"... I live."

"I tell you truly, there are some standing here
who will not taste death before they see
the kingdom of God."

(Luke 9:27)

Meditation 23 - Welcoming

A welcoming heart
is a playground for God.
To welcome God
requires a playful soul,
full of curiosity,
quick to delight,
and flexible enough
to crawl through tunnels
and climb in trees.

Reflections

Today I want you to do something playful and silly. Swing, slide, run, dance, laugh, cavort with your dog, play a game of cards by yourself or with friends, go bowling, play golf, shuffleboard, football, basketball—anything as long as it is fun and has no sense of "should" or "ought" attached. Do it now! No, now!

Breath Prayer 23

Breathe in:
"Come God ..."
Breathe out:
"... play with me."

"Anyone who welcomes this little child in my name
welcomes me; and anyone who welcomes me,
welcomes the one who sent me."

(Luke 9:48)

Meditation 24 - Greatest

Greatest and least,
least and greatest.
The words lose their meaning
to the person of the Word.
Interchangeable words,
each contained within the other,
as the tree is in the acorn
and the acorn in the tree.
Don't give a thought
to greatest
or to least.

Reflections
An exercise: Consider the most menial task you have to do today as the most important. Give it your full attention and reverence and do it as if the world were watching. Likewise consider the most important task as the most menial. Do it well but remember that in the grand scheme of things it has no importance. Practice this switch often and notice the wonderful changes in your happiness.

Breath Prayer 24

Breathe in:
"I am the least ..."
Breathe out:
"... I am the greatest."
(Repeat until the words lose
their power of distinction.)

"The least among you all
is the one who is the greatest."

(Luke 9:48)

Meditation 25 - Us

Us
Them
Them
Us
There are no 'them'
in the kingdom of God.
There is only 'us.'
Even those who openly declare
that they are not,
nor will they ever be,
'us,'
and we who declare in turn
that we are not,
nor will we ever be
'them,'
are the same beloved of God.
What God has made one
do not divide in two.

Reflections

Of course you like some people better than others. Everyone does. That should not create a "them" mentality. If you are surrounded by people who are "wrong" in everything they say and do, it is time to examine the categories within your own mind.

Breath Prayer 25

Breathe in:
"I am the same ..."
Breathe out:
"... as you."

[To his disciples who were worried about a stranger healing in Jesus' name, Jesus replied,] "You must not stop him; anyone who is not against you is for you."

(Luke 9:50)

Meditation 26 - Home

The answer to the question,
"Where?"
is always
"Here!"
No particular place can be home
for the person in whom the Word dwells.
Nests and holes
fit birds and foxes.
But you must dwell with God
in the eternal now
and the omnipresent here.

Reflections

I get very homesick for my wife and my own bed whenever I travel. I enjoy the work I do leading retreats and speaking, but when evening comes I project my thoughts toward home and wish I were there. As a result I often miss the special ministry the Spirit gives to travelers; the special awareness that all the cosmos is home and that I am never alone.

Breath Prayer 26

Breathe in:
"I am here ..."
Breathe out:
"... this is home."

**Jesus answered, "Foxes have holes
and the birds of the air have nests,
but the Son of man has nowhere to lay his head."**

(Luke 9:58)

Meditation 27 - What Time Is It?

Two questions.
Two correct answers.
All you need to be blessed of God.
Where are you?
What time is it?
These two alone are wisdom.
Without them all is chasing the wind.

When you know the answers
with your body, soul, and mind,
you will see God.
For where is God? Here!
And when will God come? Now!
And where are you?
And what time is it?

Reflections

God loves you as you are, not as you wish you were. God loves
you now, not when you get your act together. God meets you
here, not somewhere more spiritual. As you are, where you are,
now! Wake up!

Breath Prayer 27

Breathe in:
"I am here ..."
Breathe out:
"... it is now."

**"The time is fulfilled and the kingdom of God
is close at hand."**

(Mark 1:15)

Meditation 28 - Correct Action

The ability to choose and act correctly
comes only from freedom,
from knowing that there is
nothing to gain
and nothing to lose.

If you calculate gain when considering an action
correct action will elude you.
If you fear loss when considering an action
correct action is impossible.
If you are one with the Word
you have no need of gain,
no fear of loss.
You will always act correctly.

Reflections
If you truly didn't need anything and truly didn't fear anything, what would you do? Where would you be living? What would you be doing with your time? Who would you be with? How would you behave during the day? Sometimes I think we hold on to our fears because we're afraid of what we might do if they weren't there to give us an excuse for inaction.

Breath Prayer 28

Breathe in:
"I need no gain ..."
Breathe out:
"... I fear no loss."

At once they left their nets and followed him.

(Mark 1:18)

Meditation 29 - Solitude

Solitude must precede speech.
Words emerge from wordlessness.
All of the recorded spoken words of Jesus
will fit in thirty pages, double spaced.

He prepared for thirty years
to speak these words.
It is the silence of Jesus
that we must hear.
In the quiet he heard the Living Word
and in the quiet so shall we.

Reflections

What's a good ratio of silence to speech for a healthy spiritual
life? I would venture to guess it was at least 10 days of silence
and reflection to every 10 minutes of speech for Jesus. What's
your ratio? Why?

Breath Prayer 29

Breathe in:
"Come ..."
Breathe out:
"... to the quiet."

In the morning, long before dawn, he got up
and left the house, and went off to a
lonely place and prayed there.

(Mark 1:35)

Meditation 30 - Containers

Religion will never contain spirituality.
Concepts of God will never hold God.
Words about the Word will forever fall short.

As you sit in mindful meditation
you create each moment a new vessel,
a new container for the Word.
In the next moment it is broken
and you must create all over again.
This is the proper practice
of the Presence of God.

Reflections
An old Chinese proverb says, "Renew yourself again each day, and again, and again, and again." Who you thought you were yesterday is not a fit container for who you are becoming today. Everything is new.

Breath Prayer 30

Breathe in:
"Make my heart ..."
Breathe out:
"... new each day."

"Nobody puts new wine into old wineskins."

(Mark 2:22)

Meditation 31 - Rules

Rules are like supports
placed around a young tree
while it sinks its roots
deep into nourishing soil
before reaching for the sun.
But these supports are not the tree.

It is the nature of a tree
to drink deeply of the soil
and to stretch out for the sun,
not to lean on supports.

It is your nature
to drink deeply of your soul
and to stretch out for God,
not to follow rules.

Reflections
Should I break the rules, then? Come on now. Just stop
worrying about all the technicalities and beating up on yourself.
The law is written in the very nature of your being. Stretch out
for God. The rest will come naturally.

Breath Prayer 31

Breathe in:
"I drink deep ..."
Breathe out:
"... I reach high."

**"The Sabbath was made for man,
not man for the Sabbath."**

(Mark 2:27)

Meditation 32 - Division

God cannot be divided against God.

Devils are creations of our divided mind.

In the Word there are no divisions.

Therefore a person of the Word

is extremely cautious in making judgments

and distinctions,

dividing into "good"

and "bad."

Such distinctions come from the ego's

limited awareness.

God is good.

God is the ultimate reality.

Stop creating the very evil you fear.

Heal your divided mind

and you will heal the world.

Reflections

The greatest battle being fought is the one within your mind. God has no need of fighting battles. Be very very careful of dividing people into categories of "friends" and "enemies." You can't see things from God's perspective. Don't think that God has "enemies." Enemies exist only when there is some sort of threat. Nothing threatens God.

Breath Prayer 32

Breathe in:
"Hear, O my soul ..."
Breathe out:
"... God is One."

**"If a kingdom is divided against itself
that kingdom cannot last."**

(Mark 3:24)

Meditation 33 - Growing

God did not merely "make" the cosmos.
God is growing the cosmos.
Everything is growing
in its own way,
at its own speed.
The Word is not making you
into something you are not...
It is growing you
into that which
you are.

Reflections
The Chinese have a phrase, "Wu wei." It means,"effortless doing." It is the kind of work that takes place naturally. Great things are accomplished but there is no strain or tension. Great power is manifested but no force is necessary. Stop pulling up your roots to see if you are growing. You are doing fine.

Breath Prayer 33

Breathe in:
"I am becoming ..."
Breathe out:
"... who I am."

"This is what the kingdom of God is like.
A man scatters seed on the land. Night and day,
while he sleeps, when he is awake,
the seed is sprouting and growing."

(Mark 4:26-27)

Meditation 34 - Lamp

All the light you need to find your path,
and to make your way along that path,
has been provided for you.

God did not light the lamp of life
and then hide its glow.
All persons have within
the light they need
to see the road ahead.

But you must be mindful.
Mindfulness is like eyes that are open wide,
that see all light and shadow.
To live without mindfulness
is to close the eyes
and darken the light provided.

Reflections

Pay gentle attention to all the ordinary things around you. Every hummingbird, every breeze blowing leaves across the road, every piece of music in the air, every smile and every frown—all together provide the message of the present moment which is all you need to take the next step. Look around right now. Listen! Smell! Be aware! There is light everywhere.

Breath Prayer 34

Breathe in:
"Light of God ..."
Breathe out:
"... show me the path."

"Is a lamp brought in to be put under a tub,
or under the bed?"

(Mark 4:21)

Meditation 35 - Worry

If you are able to stop thinking
about the past,
it no longer exists.
If you are able to stop thinking
about the future,
it no longer exists.
Only the present moment exists.

Do you see, then,
all regrets,
all worries,
are merely products
of a physical mind.
They do not threaten God,
neither need they threaten you.

Reflections
I know people for whom prayer is just a long list of worries
brought before God. In order to truly stop worrying you have to
stop wanting things to be or to go a certain way.

Breath Prayer 35

Breathe in:
"The past is past ..."
Breathe out:
"... the future is illusion."

**"Do not worry about tomorrow,
tomorrow will take care of itself."**

(Matthew 6:34)

Meditation 36 - Eternal Life

Don't look for eternal life
as a reward for pious living.
Don't expect it to be
a continuation of the ego's illusions.
Don't seek to find it
at the end of some journey.

It is here, now.
You need only stop and know it.
Know it from an inner knowing.
And in that knowing,
you will know God.
And in <u>that</u> knowing,
you will know all life.

Reflections

Look at yourself. You are alive! Yet every atom in your body has been replaced in the past ten years. Not one atom is the same! Yet something is still the same. What is it? What are you? When you can answer that, you can live.

Breath Prayer 36

Breathe in:
"I know ..."
Breathe out:
"... I am alive."

"And eternal life is this: to know you, the only true God, and Jesus Christ whom you have sent."

(John 17:3)

Meditation 37 - Letting Go

Every form lets go of itself
that a new form might emerge.
A log lets go of itself
to become fire.
The sun lets go of itself
to become energy and warmth.
This moment lets go of itself
to become the next.
The whole of creation is one glorious act
of letting go to greater things.
Why do you hold on?

Reflections

The tiny, tiny bit of reality you have sensed through your five senses has been mistakenly used by your brain to construct a view of "how things really are." The only way to experience real life is by letting go of each moment and opening to what the next moment brings. The tighter you hold on, the less you live. What are you clinging to now?

Breath Prayer 37

Breathe in:
"Letting ..."
Breathe out:
"... go."

"In all truth I tell you, unless a wheat grain
falls into the earth and dies, it remains only a
single grain, but if it dies, it yields a rich harvest."

(John 12:24)

Meditation 38 - Stones

We hate the sins of others
in direct proportion
to their power
in our own subconscious shadow.
Learn to know the secret places
of your heart.
With courage
bring them to the light,
and compassion will replace judgment
and stones will lie unused
upon the ground.

Reflections

Every critical thought you have is born of fear of your own shadow. You are afraid that if you do not judge others that the demons of your own heart will get loose. Don't be afraid. God sees the depths of your heart and does not judge. As you stop judging you will be free to bring things to the light and the light will dissolve them.

Breath Prayer 38

Breathe in:
"No stones ..."
Breathe out:
"... will I throw."

**"Let the one among you who is guiltless
be the first to throw a stone at her."**

(John 8:7)

Meditation 39 - I Am

Seeing time unfold before you,
one moment following another,
some things before,
others after,
is only one way of seeing.
It is a way of seeing
that is fashioned by our mind.
But our spirit knows another
deeper way of seeing,
in which time is an ocean,
not a river.
When you dive into that ocean
you will know
that you are as eternal
as Abraham.

Reflections

Don't be afraid of your own eternal nature. It is a gift of the Image of God within you. You are not being grandiose when you realize, "I am." You are discovering your true nature. You are not trying to be God. You are sinking into the realization that the Image of God within you is a reality and not just a metaphor. Remember: You are.

Breath Prayer 39

Breathe in:
"I ..."
Breathe out:
"... am!"

"In all truth I tell you, before Abraham was,
I am."

(John 8:58)

Meditation 40 - Guidance

When you wonder which way to turn,
confused by the many choices,
paralyzed by fears of futures unknown;
When choices have collapsed
and the way ahead has vanished;
When you feel trapped
in a painful present
stretching into eternity
with no way out;
Then the voice you must listen to
and the guidance you must follow
will be inside of you.
It will speak from your heart.
It will be hard to hear
because you have been taught to listen outside,
to trust others.
But if you listen carefully,
and patiently,
you will hear
and you will know.

Reflections

Go ahead and ask others for advice if you sense they rely on the same Source as you. But don't worry if they only add to your confusion and doubt. You will eventually sense within you the Source of all answers. When you finally understand how and where to go for guidance the answer will be self-evident.

Breath Prayer 40

Breathe in:
"The Lord ..."
Breathe out:
"... is my shepherd."

"I am the good shepherd,
I know my own and my own know me."

(John 10:14)

Meditation 41 - Poor In Spirit

You are a person of the soil.
Your material being comes from
and returns to
earth.
How marvelous!
Dirt,
filled with Spirit,
dances on the earth
from which it came
and to which it returns.

Incarnated Spirit
but still of the earth.
Happy to remember your origins
both in heaven
and in earth.
Heavenly person of earth,
earthly person of heaven.

Reflections

Don't be discouraged with your poor body. It will have its aches, pains, and limitations and will eventually die. This is as it should be. Recognize that you are temporarily holding energy together in this particular form. You will soon move on to another form. Knowing this, you neither despise nor overvalue this form. Earth goes back to earth. Spirit is eternal.

Breath Prayer 41

Breathe in:
"Earth ..."
Breathe out:
"... I am!"

"How blessed are the poor in spirit:
the kingdom of Heaven is theirs."

(Matthew 5:3)

Meditation 42 - Gentle

How difficult to impose your way,
your path,
your views,
your desires
on another person.
What struggle,
what hardship,
what heartache.

Much easier and wiser to let others
go their own way,
feel their own feelings,
think their own thoughts,
yet still keep them
in the center of your heart.

Love,
not control,
is the way of the Word.

Reflections

People have the annoying tendency to do what they want rather than what we think they should do, believe what they want rather than what we think they should believe, and feel what they feel rather than what we think they should feel. You can use this fact to keep yourself forever frustrated if you wish. Or you can get on with living the life God has for you.

Breath Prayer 42

Breathe in:
"I release ..."
Breathe out:
"... you."

"Blessed are the gentle,
they shall have the earth as inheritance."

(Matthew 5:4)

Meditation 43 - Mourn

To attempt to gain
without losing,
arrive
without leaving,
laugh
without crying,
fill
without emptying,
believe
without doubting,
or
live
without dying
is to be forever frustrated.

God encompasses all opposites.
To live happily in God
you must fully live both sides.

Reflections

One of the most common maladies I see among Christians in my practice is the repression of negative emotions and thoughts. There seems to be a cultural taboo that states that Christians must never fall victim to negative or "bad" thoughts. On the contrary, they must be fully felt in order to be processed and integrated into a healthy personality.

Breath Prayer 43

Breathe in:
"I live ..."
Breathe out:
"... I die!"
Breathe in:
"I laugh ..."
Breathe out:
"... I cry."

"Blessed are those who mourn,
they shall be comforted"

(Matthew 5:5)

Meditation 44 - Hunger

Every preacher,
every moralist,
every politician
will gladly tell you
what is right.
If you fill yourself with their food,
you will satiate your mind
but starve your soul.

The empty calories
of easy answers
served up by others
will not nurture.

Remain hungry.
Stay dissatisfied
until pure food appears
from deep within your spirit.
Then eat your fill
and you will be satisfied.

Reflections

Culture will tell you that the good life is the life that arranges circumstances so that gain far exceeds loss. Wrong! The good life comes to those who are dissatisfied with anything less than the solid food of God, given to all who seek.

Breath Prayer 44

Breathe in:
"Feed me ..."
Breathe out:
"... holy food."

**"Blessed are those who hunger and thirst
for uprightness, they shall have their fill."**

(Matthew 5:6)

Meditation 45 - Ambition

The ambitious mind seeks objectives.
The fearful mind seeks enemies.
The desirous mind seeks treasures.
The dissatisfied mind creates idols for itself.

The soul has no ambition,
nothing to fear,
nothing to desire
and nothing to seek.
Can you polish the inner mirror of your mind
until it reflects nothing but Light?

Reflections
Purity is not externally defined. Purity is the ability to be content
with that which comes from God, nothing else being necessary.
Don't try to become pure. God has made your soul pure and
holy. Stop trying to add things to your life.

Breath Prayer 45

Breathe in:
"My soul ..."
Breathe out:
"... is pure!"

"Blessed are the pure in heart:
they shall see God."

(Matthew 5:8)

Meditation 46 - Salt

Don't try to be Jesus.

Jesus was Jesus.

Don't try to be St. Francis.

Francis was Francis.

Be you!

No one else can.

That about you

which you judge as unacceptable

is part of what gives you

your unique flavor.

Be careful of self improvement efforts.

You may be trying to be something you are not.

If you become fully who you are,

flaws and blemishes,

gifts and graces,

you will give your taste to the world.

Reflections

Have you ever given thanks for the mistakes you have made? They are part of you. This is the very paradox with which Paul struggled. "Should I make more mistakes then that I can learn even more?" Relax. This paradox resolves itself naturally. Each mistake accepted and integrated into our being cleanses us and frees us from making that mistake again. Each mistake repressed and avoided dooms us to repeat it. You are who you are and you have done what you have done. That is the person God loves.

Breath Prayer 46

Breathe in:

"I am ..."

Breathe out:

"... me."

"You are the salt of the earth."

(Matthew 5:13)

Meditation 47 - Light

Why do you search for the light?
Why do you pray for illumination?
Why do you beg God to show God's face?

Nothing is being witheld from you.
God is not hiding from you.
The Light is within,
shining in your own heart.

Stop pretending that you
are nothing but a miserable sinner.
That game has helped you hide
from yourself and God.

Stop hiding.
People are waiting
to see the light of God.

Reflections

Go stand in front of the mirror, now. And look intently into the reflection of your eyes. Does it make you comfortable or uncomfortable? May I suggest that your spiritual discipline for the next few days or weeks be to look into your own eyes for 10 to 15 minutes each day until you truly understand that you are looking into the very image of God. If you can't learn to see God there, you will never see God outside.

Breath Prayer 47

Breathe in:
"I am   ..."
Breathe out:
"... light."

"You are the light of the world."

(Matthew 5:14)

Meditation 48 - Law

Do not be afraid of the Law.
It is not what people have claimed.
It is the essence of who you are.
It is written in your very atomic structure.
It binds together all that is.
You cannot move away from it.
You cannot escape it.

But never fear.
How can that which is written
with the Pen of Love
bring you harm?
It exists to guide you home.
And it will do that without fail.

Reflections

Jeremiah said in Chapter 31:33 that the law will be "written on our hearts." How could Jesus abolish that which is written into our very nature? All pain comes from thinking that the law is written on stone or on paper. If you live from your heart, you will keep the law, I guarantee it. Now the primary question is: "How do I truly live from my heart?"

Breath Prayer 48

Breathe in:
"Word of God ..."
Breathe out:
"... take me home."

"Do not imagine that I have come
to abolish the Law or the Prophets."

(Matthew 5:17)

Meditation 49 - Perfection

If you try to always do it right
you will be forever frustrated.
Your mind is divided
and judges yourself and others
continually.

You must step aside from your own mind.
You must not worry about perfection.
Only God is perfect.
Stop trying to do it the way others
insist is right.

God lives within you.
Live there yourself
and God will do
your doing for you.
It will be a perfectly effortless doing.

Reflections

Hear this and hear it well: There is nothing wrong with you!
Until you can truly believe that, you will continue to try to do it
right and you will continue to fail. This is the great paradox of
our faith: When I quit trying to be perfect, God perfects His love
within me. Don't dismiss this and don't try to rationally figure it
out. Meditate upon it for a few months and see.

Breath Prayer 49

Breathe in:
"I am perfect   ..."
Breathe out:
"... as I am."

———————————————

**"You must therefore set no bounds to your love,
just as your heavenly Father sets none to his."**

(Matthew 5:48)

Meditation 50 - Charity

Of more importance
than the size of your check
is the size of your heart.

God has no need of your money.
Giving is only a means
to enlarge your heart,
reduce your fears,
quiet your mind,
and free you from worry.

Reward enough?

Reflections

God will accomplish God's purposes whether you give or not.
Count on it. God desires your charity so that Love may flow
through the hidden recesses of your heart and nourish your soul.
The more you give, the less fear you have. The less fear you have,
the happier you are. The happier you are, the more you give.
Wonderful circle, isn't it?

Breath Prayer 50

Breathe in:
"I give ..."
Breathe out:
"... in secret."

"Your almsgiving must be secret, and your father
who sees all that is done in secret
will reward you."

(Matthew 6:4)

Meditation 51 - Private

Conversation with God is a private matter.
It cannot be a performance
before an audience,
even the audience of your own mind.

Shut your eyes.
Shut your ears.
Turn off the endless stream of words
flowing through your consciousness.
Breathe slowly and calmly.
Relax your body.

There is no one to impress here.
Neither other people
nor your own critical ego.
Here there is only God.

Is this enough?

Reflections
Who is watching you when you pray? No one, you say? Think
again. Usually we have some image in the back of our mind,
some audience who is evaluating, criticizing, monitoring our
words, making sure we do it "right." "Should I pray for this?"
"I'm not really worthy to ask." "Is this really working?" "I can't
say that!" So it goes, an endless commentary. You don't have to
do it right. Just sit there until all the voices quiet down. No
audiences in the mind. Just you and God.

Breath Prayer 51

Breathe in:
"I am quiet   ..."
Breathe out:
"... in your presence."

"But when you pray, go to your private room,
shut yourself in, and so pray to your Father
who is in that secret place."

(Matthew 6:6)

Meditation 52 - Pearls

Your mind will seek
to tame your soul.

The wild and wonderful soul
will show you adventure,
and the mind will call it danger.
The soul will show you peace,
and the mind will call it boredom.
The soul will bring you love,
and the mind will call it dependency.
The soul will create compassion,
and the mind will call it weakness.
The soul will introduce you to eternal life,
and the mind will call it death.

Whom do you believe?

Reflections

There is nothing "bad" about your mind. It has just created the illusion that it is who you are. Wrong! It is merely your central processing unit (CPU). It is no more who you are than is the CPU of your computer. It is a physical, limited computer. It processes information delivered by your senses and arranges it in some order, therefore creating a particular view of the world. As wonderful a mechanism as it is, it is very limited in the view it has constructed. If the mind is your "CPU" then your Soul is the programmer, the real you. Don't get the two mixed up.

Breath Prayer 52

Breathe in:
"I trust ..."
Breathe out:
"... my soul."

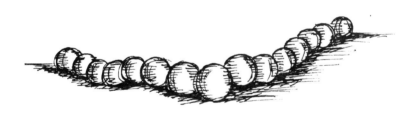

"Do not throw your pearls in front of pigs."

(Matthew 7:6)